Help Me With The 90%

by

Kevin & Laura Hinnant

Dreams Publishing Company
Post Office Box 4731
Rocky Mount, North Carolina 27803
www.DreamsPublishing.com

Designed by Larry Russell for Nicki Angela

Manufactured in the United States of America

ISBN 0-9770936-9-7

Library of Congress Control Number (LCCN): 2007923485
1. Self-Help – Non-Fiction
2. Finances - Money
3. Religious Teaching

Special Thanks

First and foremost, we thank God for allowing us the opportunity, through wisdom and knowledge to write this book. If it wasn't for His grace, which to us means the ability to do what you ordinary could not do; it couldn't be possible.

It's with joy that we would like to thank our parents, Verna Mae Jimmerson, Ivory & Janice Hinnant, our family, and our friends for always having a loving and encouraging word as we continued to grow stronger in the Lord. We thank each of you for the prayers that have gone up on our behalf. You are the most precious gift that anyone can wish for. We pray that God will continue to bless each of you abundantly.

To Mintus & Barbara Campbell for sowing that seed of a $150.00 in our lives on March 21, 2001. Also for believing in us during our most difficult times, even when we didn't believe in ourselves. Your love and encouragement means more to us than you will ever no. Thank you, even today, for your mentoring and prays always.

To Cathy Farmer for being a leader that pushes the people of God to walk in their assignment. We thank you for praying for us, for pushing us, for mentoring us, for encouraging us, for believing in us, and for loving us for who we are. The messages you ministered to us on faith, trust, family, finances, wisdom, and knowledge, will always be in our mind and heart. Those messages always let us know that by allowing God to lead us and be in His perfect will, we can accomplish everything He has set before us.

With Many Blessings
Kevin and Laura

Foreword

When God has a plan for your life, there is a process He takes you through which at first is hard to understand. But if you yield to the process, you will begin to see that it will all work out for your good.

So it is with this couple, Kevin and Laura Hinnant. They found themselves going through financial pain. The pain that they went through has become their passion and ministry. It's a driving force in their lives to help others come out of financial bondage. Once you've been set free, you have a desire to see others set free.

We praise God for what He has done in this couple. They received the financial principles that were taught and allowed reformation to take place in them. We saw their lives transform as they applied the principles of financial success to their lives.

We encourage you to read this book that has been birthed out of them and begin to allow reformation to take place in your life.

They have helped many people get on the road to financial success by teaching them to budget and become good stewards over the 90% that remains after you have presented the first 10% to God.

They encourage couples to come in unity with their finances so that God can move mightily in their lives.

We thank God for you, Kevin and Laura Hinnant, and for the awesome work you are doing in the Kingdom of God.

God Bless You
Pastor Barbara Campbell
Higher Elevation Ministries
Goldsboro, North Carolina

Table of Contents

Broken Down and Built Back Up

Our Testimony

Have you ever had a year that you want to forget? One you *don't* want to forget? I am quite sure that for the average person, the answer would be yes.

For our family, there are two such years: 1999 and 2000. Those years are when God broke us all the way down to the ground, so that He could build us back up – build us back up in His image. Build us back up so we would know without a shadow of a doubt that God – and only God – is the head of our lives. The head of everything we do. The head of everything with which He has entrusted us.

The Rebuilding Process

Kevin:

Our rebuilding process began on May 19, 1999, just a day after our youngest daughter, Pashion, was born. I left my wife's hospital room to go pick up my monthly commission check from work. I remember telling Laura that I was going to fill her room with flowers and teddy bears.

Well, that didn't happen. I came back with one little teddy bear and a few pieces of candy; the commission check that should have totaled four thousand, five hundred dollars was, to my shock, only issued for four hundred and fifty-eight dollars. Worse still, the paycheck had not been issued in error. It was in that amount because of charge-backs: several of my customers hadn't paid their bills. When that happens, the company has the right to charge that amount back to you; and in this case it did. As you can imagine, the timing for us could not have been worse. Why now?

We can look back and think, *if only we had been serving God totally and saving, like we knew God wanted us to, we wouldn't have received such a great financial setback.* But because we didn't have a solid spiritual relationship with God, or any real understanding of savings, we had set ourselves up for failure.

Laura:

I will never forget that day when Kevin came back to my room with only a small teddy bear in his hands. I knew immediately that something had happened – something to do with the commission check. I knew we were in trouble from the look of distress, disbelief, and failure on Kevin's face. It was a look that I don't ever want to see again.

Things were okay between us during the time I was in the hospital. We had to maintain a standard and not let our family and friends know we were headed straight for trouble. But we were; and not just financially, but with our marriage and with each other.

When I checked out and went home, everything was still okay. We still had my paychecks on which to fall back. Several months before the baby came, Kevin's job situation had changed. He was no longer traveling from state to state, but decided instead to build his clientele in North Carolina. This, too, caused the money to slow down; the big commission checks had stopped, but the problems had only just begun.

Would the Marriage Last?

Laura:

There were periods of silence. Periods of frustration. Periods of me wanting to go back to Mississippi. Periods of Kevin wanting me to go back to Mississippi. We begin to blame each other for the financial problems. You see, we had spent a lot of money on clothes, shoes, eating out, and other material things. We never saved a dime. We had to keep up our lifestyle of having material things and not having to ask anyone for anything. Oh, we didn't even tithe, let alone give any amount of money that mattered to the church.

Kevin:

I remember every time Laura got paid or received some money, she would get mad at the situation all over again. She began telling me that she was the head of the household, that she brought in the bacon, so to speak. She would say that she was the only one working at a real job and that she could do what she wanted with her money.

That didn't make me feel too good. I remember thinking that she was the one who had wanted me to stop working out of state so that I would be home. Even though I worked other jobs, nothing came close to the income I had left. My income for that period was about one-quarter of what it had been.

I even remember one time when I was walking out to the mailbox, I stood there waiting for the traffic to clear, and the thought came – *why not just step out in front of that truck? You are worthless anyway. You have no money, your wife thinks you are a failure, everyone would be better off without you.* I believe the only reason I was able to cast that thought out from my imagination was that I immediately thought, *if I do, who will take care of Kevin, Jr.? The girls have their mother, but who will take care of him?*

Now I thank God that, no matter what temptations may come your way, He always gives a pathway of escape. One thing we can say is that our marriage was definitely put through a test, but by the grace of God, our marriage was saved. A marriage that's now filled with love, trust, understanding, and respect.

Bill Collectors

Kevin:

As the months went by, bill collectors began calling every day. Instead of talking to them and telling them about our situation, we avoided any perceived awkwardness by looking at Caller ID and not answering the phone. This in turn made them come after us even more. What we *should* have done was give our life and all situations totally to God. But no – we tried to handle the situation ourselves. We continued to make things into a bigger mess.

At that time, I drove a burgundy Ford Explorer and Laura drove a burgundy Plymouth Breeze. Both cars were voluntarily repossessed – yes, both cars. We didn't have anything to drive. We believe now that this was when the rebuilding process really began.

My mom, Janice, let us use her white car, a color that Laura had said she would *never* drive, but now she was humbled. We would leave the house around 6:30 in the morning and drive about thirty-five minutes to pick Mom up so she wouldn't be late for work. Then I would drop Laura off at work and then I would go to work. Mom allowed us to use her car for about six months and she never complained or asked us for anything in return, not even to make a payment.

After that, our cousin Rudolph gave us our first Volvo. It was a gray 1982 two-door sedan. We drove that car for a few weeks … until it had engine trouble.

I'll never forget the night when the car broke down. We were going home from church at about 11:30 p.m. By this time, we were going back to church more regularly. We stayed on a country road about ten miles off the main highway. God was working once again in our lives. There were only two areas of houses on that road, and, by the grace of God, the car stopped right in from of the only house that had a light on. God was taking care of us, and we didn't even recognize it. The man who lived there took us home. When we got home, it was so quiet in there, you could have heard a pin drop. Our niece, Veronica Jimmerson was staying with us and all she asked us was if we wanted her to put Pashion down for bed. She was always so helpful to us during our hard times, which didn't give the children a time to think about things that would cause them to ask any questions. They were so great during that time.

Pride, Again?

Kevin:

In the meantime, we were now without a vehicle again! For the next few weeks we didn't want to ask anyone for anything, so we drove an old church van provided by Cousin Rudolph. It was corroded on the bottom where the road salt had eaten away at the metal. This was during the winter, and it had no heat. It also developed a problem with the transmission and wouldn't go into reverse.

Of course, it just had to snow.

One Monday morning, we got stuck in the front yard trying to turn the van around, which was difficult to do since it wouldn't go in reverse. So there we were: Laura was steering and I was shoveling ice and snow from under the tires, trying to get traction. As Laura was sitting there in the front seat, she was thinking, *why does he have me living like this, I don't care where he is trying to go, I'm just sick and tired of living this way.*

So there we were, in need of transportation again. Who stepped in? God did. Our guardian angel, Mom Janice, once again let us use her car a couple more months. We began going to church, to Sunday school, and to Bible study; we started tithing, reading our Bible, and having a real relationship with God.

After that, our Cousin Rudolph gave us another car. It was an off-white 1979 Volvo. That Volvo! Laura wasn't too fond of that car. She wasn't grateful because, according to her, the car looked like it had been through a hundred accidents. The paint was corroded and she just didn't want to be seen in it.

Laura:

I would have Kevin take me to work early and I would stay late to make sure all my coworkers were gone from the parking lot before calling Kevin to pick me up. You see, I didn't want anyone seeing me get in that car. I still had too much pride and I was too arrogant.

The Truth Is Revealed

Laura:

One day back in November of 1999 while I was at work, my very good friend Senora came over to my desk. We begin talking and she asked me whether or not I was going home to Mississippi to see my mom for Christmas. I told her no; and she remarked that it seemed strange, since she remembered I hadn't gone home for Mother's Day, either, or during the summer; and at that moment I burst into tears. I told her everything – I mean *everything*. That we didn't have a car. That Kevin was working odd jobs and we didn't have any food to eat – not just for a couple of days, but for three whole months, on and off. During that time, we did our best to make sure the children ate. I began telling her things that even our church family didn't know, things that our own families didn't know, things we never talked about because we had too much pride. And then, once again, God moved on our behalf.

I didn't expect what happened next. Later that evening, Senora asked me to call Kevin and for us to come to her house after work. When we got there, both of her cars were filled with bags and boxes of groceries, toys and clothes for the kids. We couldn't believe what God had done through the helping hands of Senora and a few co-workers.

Did the Problems Stop?

Laura:

We have to remember that the problems we create don't stop just because we decide to let God take control of our lives. We had a process to go through, and go through in God's way.

One day while at Mom's house just lounging around, I decided to go around the corner to my sister-in-law Barbara's house. She was eating a chocolate moon-pie. You're probably wondering what a moon-pie has to do with anything; you'll see. I asked her for a piece of her moon-pie and she wouldn't give me any. I asked again and again, and she still didn't give me a piece. I had pride; and she didn't know that I was actually not joking and that I was really hungry. She didn't give me any, and when she put that last piece of moon-pie in her mouth, I ran out the house crying and angry. I just couldn't believe that she wouldn't give me any.

All I could think of was that during the time when I thought I was on top of the world, I let her use my car any time she asked. I gave her money, food – anything she asked for. And now that I needed something from her, she refused to give me what I asked for.

You see I was putting my trust in people to help me, and not putting my trust in the only man who *could* help us. That man's name is Jesus Christ. I went back to Mom's house, still crying. My family asked what was wrong and I told them about the moon-pie. I remember someone saying that I was just too sensitive. I ran out of there again – really, really crying now. All I could think of was that if I had had a gun, I would have shot Barbara.

Now, that's an incredibly bad feeling to have about someone. But you know what? Barbara and I were in God's hands, because God would have never let my mind carry out that terrible thought.

Then God sent another angel to me, my sister-in-law Andrea. She began to ask me what was really wrong. I wouldn't shed any light on why I'd reacted the way I did. All I kept saying is that I was hungry and that we didn't have any food. She thought I was just hungry for that day. I still didn't tell her anything about our situation. I had too much pride, and didn't want our family to know what was going on.

Andrea began to minister to me in the Spirit, but I didn't want to hear what she was saying. She told me that we needed to start trusting in God and that we should stop putting our trust in our jobs. She told me that we were running from God and what He had for us to do in His Kingdom. I remember just walking off from her, still crying about *my* situation. I didn't want to hear anything she was saying. But what I also remember is her not giving up. She continued to talk about Jesus and how if we let Him, He would begin to guide our every thought, our lives, our finances, etc. She also took me to the store and bought me a whole box of moon-pies and some chocolate milk.

I remember that it was in the following week that several family members began to figure out that we had a serious problem … that we really did need help. They didn't know to what extent, but they knew that we needed our family. That following Tuesday afternoon, our daughter Lakisha came running to get me, saying, "Mom, look at all this food Aunt Arlene and Uncle Ricky bought us!" She also wanted to know why they were bringing us all this food. I remember her making a joke and saying, "now you don't have to go to the grocery store." What she didn't know was that we didn't have the money to go to the grocery store or to any other store.

The next week, Kevin's brother Kendrick and his wife Andrea (the angel) also bought us many bags of groceries out to the house. The blessings just kept coming in. But I wasn't even grateful. I even told them I was going to pay them back when I got paid, even knowing full well that I couldn't pay them back. See, pride was still a factor in my life. Their bringing us food was perhaps something small, but our family's show of love really made a difference in the next few months of our lives.

Kevin:

We felt it was time to tell Laura's family in Mississippi. She called her sister Jean and told her everything. Jean asked her why we didn't tell them that we needed help. You see, Laura has the kind of loving family that would have sent us their last dime. But they would have worried every day about us, about what the children were eating, about us not having a car to get to work. They probably would have borrowed some money to send us. They are just that kind of generous and caring family. We love them dearly.

At the end of the conversation, we told them that we were going to be okay and that our lives had made a turn for the better. The truth was finally out: we could now stop pretending. But do you know what? Everything really was okay, because we were finally trusting in our faith.

Did We Give In To the Enemy?

Laura:

During this time, we lost a mobile home that Kevin had owned prior to our marriage. We lost two cars and many other material things. We sat in the dark because we didn't have money to pay the light bill. The phone service was cut off. We almost lost the home in which we were living. For days at a time, we didn't have food to eat. We didn't have money to buy gas. We didn't have money to give to the church or money which to bless anyone. We just didn't have any extra after we gave our tithe.

But we didn't give in to the enemy. We continued to push forward, because true deliverance was right around the corner for us. The end was in sight!

Putting Our Trust Only In God

Laura:

At that time we began to serve God wholeheartedly. We began taking the entire family to church and we just began to change our entire mindset. We began to focus on the things of God … and, when we did, things began to happen that we simply couldn't explain. By this time, we were taking a School of Ministry class in Kinston, North Carolina, under the leadership of Doris Bynum. The teacher was Barbara Campbell, and the class was on John Avangini's *30, 60, Hundredfold (Financial Harvest)* book.

Through the class, we began to grasp the concept of sowing and reaping. Even though we had told our family and a couple of friends about our situation, we had not yet told the church family, because of pride. God began to minister through Pastor Barbara and something hit me (the Holy Spirit). With permission, I began sharing our testimony, our breakthrough.

God moved on Pastor Barbara the next day to bless us financially, not because she thought we needed it (*which we did*), but because she had the love of God. She sowed a seed into our lives and, from that moment on, we began sowing more, and we have reaped a harvest that is beyond our wildest dreams.

The Inspiration

Kevin:

Help Me With The 90% came about because of an experience we had one day in church, several years after God had completely changed our concept of handling money. As I looked around at the people of God, I observed many things. I saw some people giving God praise, some were dancing, singing and shouting, and others were speaking in tongues. In the midst of all of that, my thought was, *how many of these people, faithful as they may be, are struggling with finances the way we used to? How many of them will leave church and wonder how they are going to keep their lights on, feed their children, or even get gas in their cars, so that they can get to work next week?*

And I took the thought a step further. *How many will stop sowing into the Ministry, or even stop helping out a friend, because they can't pay their bills?* That's what we don't want to continue to see happening to our family, friends, and anyone who is trying to be a good steward of the 90% with which God has entrusted them.

I can't even begin to tell you the countless number of people with whom I have had the opportunity to talk about their finances who struggle with debt. People from various income levels and professions, people who dropped out of school as well as people with higher educational degrees. The Devil's Elaborate Bondage Trap (D.E.B.T.) has no preference as to whom it will deceive and enslave. No one is exempt from falling into this trap. School teachers, pastors, police officers, government employees, business owners, factory workers, accountants, doctors, lawyers … the list can go on and on.

We know that God has called us for this purpose: to bring to light what this devastating demon called debt is doing to His people. What you always need to keep in mind is one very important thing: no matter how much debt you are in, you can come out by managing what you have according to God's Word.

Proverbs 3 (NLT) reads, " ***1My child, never forget the things I have taught you. Store my commands in your heart, 2for they will give you a long and satisfying life. 3Never let loyalty and kindness get away from you! Wear them like a necklace; write them deep within your heart. 4Then you will find favor with both God and people, and you will gain a good reputation. 5Trust in the LORD with all your heart; do not depend on your own understanding. 6Seek his will in all you do, and he will direct your paths. 7Don't be impressed with your own***

***wisdom. Instead, fear the LORD and turn your back on evil. [8]Then
you will gain renewed health and vitality. [9]Honor the LORD with
your wealth and with the best part of everything your land produces.
[10]Then he will fill your barns with grain, and your vats will overflow
with the finest wine. [11]My child, don't ignore it when the LORD
disciplines you, and don't be discouraged when he corrects you.
[12]For the LORD corrects those he loves, just as a father corrects a
child in whom he delights. [13]Happy is the person who finds wisdom
and gains understanding. [14]For the profit of wisdom is better than
silver, and her wages are better than gold. [15]Wisdom is more
precious than rubies; nothing you desire can compare with her.
[16]She offers you life in her right hand, and riches and honor in her
left. [17]She will guide you down delightful paths; all her ways are
satisfying. [18]Wisdom is a tree of life to those who embrace her; happy
are those who hold her tightly. [19]By wisdom the LORD founded the
earth; by understanding he established the heavens. [20]By his
knowledge the deep fountains of the earth burst forth, and the clouds
poured down rain. [21]My child, don't lose sight of good planning and
insight. Hang on to them, [22]for they fill you with life and bring you
honor and respect. [23]They keep you safe on your way and keep your
feet from stumbling. [24]You can lie down without fear and enjoy
pleasant dreams. [25]You need not be afraid of disaster or the
destruction that comes upon the wicked, [26]for the LORD is your
security. He will keep your foot from being caught in a trap. [27]Do not
withhold good from those who deserve it when it's in your power to
help them. [28]If you can help your neighbor now, don't say, "Come
back tomorrow, and then I'll help you." [29]Do not plot against your
neighbors, for they trust you. [30]Don't make accusations against
someone who hasn't wronged you. [31]Do not envy violent people;
don't copy their ways. [32]Such wicked people are an abomination to
the LORD, but he offers his friendship to the godly. [33]The curse of
the LORD is on the house of the wicked, but his blessing is on the
home of the upright. [34]The LORD mocks at mockers, but he shows
favor to the humble. [35]The wise inherit honor, but fools are put to
shame!***

The most important thing we want you to get from this book is for you to trust God in all you do, regardless of how the situation looks right now. What we went through then, and what we learned from our mistakes, along with the re-building process, is what inspired us to write one of our testimonies.

This book also gives the reader the steps we used and are continuing to use as we continue to be good stewards of the 90% God gave us.

Trust God in all you do!

Yours in Christ
Kevin and Laura Hinnant, Sr.

Chapter 1:

Where Does the Money Go?

"I just don't understand where the money goes!" Have you – or someone you know – ever said that? If you have, then you are among millions of other tithing Christians who share that same problem. We want to cry out for help but either we don't know where to go … or we are too proud or embarrassed to ask for help.

In Malachi 3:10, God says that if we will give the whole tithe, then He will open up the windows of heaven and pour us out such a blessing that there is not room enough to receive it. He also says that He will rebuke the devourer for your sake and that all nations will call you blessed. Well, if God promises that, and you are a faithful and joyful Tither, then why do you still struggle financially?

God says that His people struggle because of a lack of knowledge. You can have the desire, discipline and faith necessary to be a good steward over your finances, but if you lack the knowledge necessary to do so, then you will always struggle with managing money.

I have met a lot of anointed Christians who are faithfully walking in their calling, faithfully giving tithes and beyond, and yet are still struggling financially. Why? Because they have never been taught how to properly handle the 90%.

> **James 1:5 (NIV)** says, "[5]*If any of you lacks wisdom, he should ask God, who gives generously to all without finding fault, and it will be given to him."*

We all have asked God for help in the area of finances. The question is, did you listen, and are you going to be obedient to what He tells you to do? Everything we need to know in order to be good stewards over the 90% is in the Word. What we must do is be obedient to the men and women of God whom He has anointed and appointed to instruct us in acquiring the wisdom and knowledge necessary to master finances. Believe it or not, successful personal money management involves 20% knowing what to do – and 80% *doing* what you know.

~Only Reach For What God Has For You~

If you allow others to establish your priorities, plans, and goals, you are going to be frustrated and unhappy. Remember that God has a plan for your life. Follow His plan –not your family member's, friend's, co-worker's, or anyone else's plan. Don't try to keep up with the Joneses! Because of you do, you will find yourself robbing Peter to pay Paul and all the other Disciples too.

It has been said that "when Jesus is all you've got, Jesus is all you need." But finding contentment in Him does not come naturally, because the world claims that happiness can be found by riding in the right car, wearing the right brand of shoes or designer clothing, living in an upscale neighborhood, or just eating the right food or drinking the right drink. Not so! As soon as you think you have the right one, a new one will come alone.

> **Proverbs 3:13-14** "*How blessed is the man who finds wisdom and the man who gains understanding, For her profit is better than the profit of silver and her gain better than fine gold.*"

~Are You Happily Married?~

Why do certain couples stay happily married? Is it that they are better-looking, more in love, or more passionate? No. Is it that they have fewer differences or less to fight about? I don't think so.

In fact, successful couples have the same number of disagreements as the couples who divorce. Even more interestingly, all couples disagree about the same basic issues – money, kids, sex, housework, in-laws, time … well, the list can go on and on. Two major causes of marital problems are money problems and fights about money. One difference between successful and unsuccessful couples is how they handle their differences.

Successful Christian couples disagree in a way that makes their relationship stronger. They listen to each other and agree on *all* major financial decisions. They even agree on the minor financial decision that may impact the family. They also have other skills and a positive attitude that helps them build long-term happiness and satisfaction. They have a strong prayer life filled with faith, trust, understanding, forgiveness, and love.

They are good stewards over the 90% that God has given them. They know that the money they earn and the possessions they have all actually belong to God. That, in turn, obligates them to earn, spend and manage their assets according to Scripture.

They resist temptations to borrow money. In fact, some of the most misunderstood and violated principles in God's Word are about credit – borrowing and lending. Many Christians believe that you should never borrow money. In fact they go to God's Word and try to pick individual Scripture verses that would lend themselves to that interpretation. Others operate no differently than do other people in the world; not only do they borrow, they borrow in excess; and some don't repay as agreed.

The Bible teaches us that *if* we *have to* borrow money, we should not be late in paying it back. Scripture does not prohibit borrowing; it just establishes very sound rules governing that borrowing.

There are three basic principles for using credit:

1. Credit should never be normal for God's people; and, if you borrow, never be late in making your payments.

   "The wicked borrows and does not pay back, but the righteous is gracious and gives."
   Psalm 37:21(NIV)

   "Do not withhold good from those who deserve it, when it is in your power to act. Do not say to your neighbor, "Come back later; I'll give it tomorrow"—when you now have it with you.
   Proverbs 3:27-38 (NIV)

   "Let no debt remain outstanding, except the continuing debt to love one another, for he who loves his fellowman has fulfilled the law.
   Romans 13:8 (NIV)

2. Credit should never be long-term.

   "The rich rules over the poor, and the borrower becomes the lender's slave." **Proverb 22:7**

3. Never sign surety - Proverbs 6:1-5 (NLT)

"It is poor judgment to co-sign a friend's note, to become responsible for a neighbor's debts." **Proverb 17:18**

So remember the following: don't borrow needlessly, don't borrow long-term, and don't borrow for things that are depreciable (such as Christmas presents, trips, clothing, and cars). If you can't pay the balance off monthly, stay away from the credit-card monster.

Most people are shocked to see cars on the list of things you shouldn't finance. What you need to realize is the cars are among the most expensive things we buy that depreciate in value. To depreciate means to go down in value. The day after you buy a new car you already owe more on it than it's worth.

I'm like most people; I never thought there was any other way to get a vehicle than with a car payment. Paying cash for a car wasn't something I had ever thought about. If you follow God's rules for handling finances, then in time you will be able to buy nice vehicles and pay cash for them.

For example, the average new car payment in the Unites States in November 2003, according to Edmunds.com, was $447.54 per month for over 62 months. Using these numbers ($447.54 x 62 months) the total that you will pay for a car when you finance it with payments is $27,747.48 provided you don't make any payments late. These numbers represent financing a $22,125 car with no money down at a 9% interest rate. Always remember these two things about financing;

#1 the higher the interest rate, the more you pay.

#2 the longer the term of the loan, the more you pay.

Proverbs 22:7 (MSG) *The poor are always ruled over by the rich, so don't borrow and put yourself under their power."*

When you borrow or finance, whichever you prefer to call it, you will now be ruled by that creditor until that debt is paid. Why continue to put yourself in that situation? Now keep the following in mind:

- Cars depreciate rapidly in value over the first two years.
- Millionaires don't buy new cars, they buy used cars.
- Most people who finance new cars upgrade before the car is paid for and finance the upside-down value into the next vehicle.

Here is an alternative to purchasing a car without a payment: If you were to save that $447 per month for a year then at the end of twelve months you would have $5,364. With that, you could buy a reliable, used car and not have any financed payments.

To go from where you are right now (financially) to where you want to be in the future (financially), it must begin with the renewing of your mind. What we are talking about is getting to the point that you no longer struggle with finances, bills, and creditors on a weekly, and/or monthly basis. That simply means being able to regularly pay your bills on time.

In order to begin paying your bills on time, you need to know and admit the answer to the following very important question.

What is the real reason you are struggling with your finances? *The answer is not because you don't make enough money*. Put your answer below.

____

____

____

~Married Couples Must Plan For The Future!~

Most couples are opposites and that's not by accident. We are attracted to people who complement us, not who compete with us. If a husband and wife will accept God's wisdom in this and work together, they will accomplish much more than either can alone. God will not bless a Christian husband and wife who are divided.

1 Peter 3:7 *"You husbands in the same way, live with your wives in an understanding way, as with someone weaker, since she is a woman; and show her honor as a fellow heir of the grace of life, so that your prayers will not be hindered".*

Genesis 2:24 "*For this reason a man shall leave his father and his mother, and be joined to his wife; and they shall become one flesh".*

Once a couple gets the revelation that they shall (promise) become one, they will begin to work as one. This is not to say that one can't make decisions without the other, but it does mean that selfish decisions won't be made. Becoming one doesn't happen overnight; it comes with the understanding and wisdom of God.

Another major part of planning is recognizing the difference between *your needs, wants, and desires.*

> **Matthew 6:24-34 (MSG)** [24]*You can't worship two gods at once. Loving one god, you'll end up hating the other. Adoration of one feeds contempt for the other. You can't worship God and Money both.* [25]*"If you decide for God, living a life of God-worship, it follows that you don't fuss about what's on the table at mealtimes or whether the clothes in your closet are in fashion. There is far more to your life than the food you put in your stomach, more to your outer appearance than the clothes you hang on your body.* [26]*Look at the birds, free and unfettered, not tied down to a job description, careless in the care of God. And you count far more to him than birds.* [27]*"Has anyone by fussing in front of the mirror ever gotten taller by so much as an inch?* [28]*All this time and money wasted on fashion--do you think it makes that much difference? Instead of looking at the fashions, walk out into the fields and look at the wildflowers. They never primp or shop,* [29]*but have you ever seen color and design quite like it? The ten best--dressed men and women in the country look shabby alongside them.* [30]*"If God gives such attention to the appearance of wildflowers--most of which are never even seen--don't you think he'll attend to you, take pride in you, do his best for you?* [31]*What I'm trying to do here is to get you to relax, to not be so preoccupied with getting, so you can respond to God's giving.* [32]*People who don't know God and the way he works fuss over these things, but you know both God and how he works.* [33]*Steep your life in God-reality, God-initiative, God-*

provisions. Don't worry about missing out. You'll find all your everyday human concerns will be met.

The difference between needs, wants, and desires can be illustrated by the motives behind our buying. We all need clothing. The need may be satisfied by simple, basic clothing or bargain buying. Wants may be met by buying in an upscale, fashion-trendy store. Desires may be met by buying exclusive designer labels or custom-made clothing.

Don't misunderstand: we're not saying that there is anything wrong with designer labels or expensive fashions. What we are saying is that you must be a good steward over the finances that God has entrusted to you. Every purchase should be evaluated and allowed or disallowed according to God's plan for your family.

> **1 John 2:15-16 (MSG)** *"15 Don't love the world's ways. Don't love the world's goods. Love of the world squeezes out love for the Father. 16 Practically everything that goes on in the world--wanting your own way, wanting everything for yourself, wanting to appear important--has nothing to do with the Father. It just isolates you from him."*

The first part of planning how to properly allocate your money is to know how much you have and from what sources you get it. We encourage you both to really begin discussing the family's money openly and honestly. If you aren't in agreement on how money is spent, it will continue to be an area where you will have arguments and disagreements. Money problems are one of the biggest reasons of divorce in America. Don't allow it to cause problems in your marriage.

Chapter 2:

The Tithe

As Christians, we should be faithful and joyful Tithers. If you are having financial problems, the first thing you must ask yourself is, "am I faithfully giving (or paying – I don't care what you call it, just do it!) the tithe?" Are you giving your tithes and offering, or are you cheating God out of what is rightly His?

> **Malachi 3:8-10** *"Should people cheat God? Yet you have cheated me! "But you ask, 'What do you mean? When did we ever cheat you?' "You have cheated me of the tithes and offerings due to me. Bring all the tithes into the storehouse so there will be enough food in my Temple. If you do says the Lord Almighty, "I will open the windows of heaven for you. I will pour out a blessing so great you won't have room to take it in! Try it! Let me prove it to you!"*

Now, don't misunderstand: God doesn't need the money! The tithe is to teach us to be givers and to not depend on money, but depend instead on Him.

> **Luke 16:13 (NIV)** *"No servant can serve two masters. Either he will hate the one and love the other, or he will be devoted to the one and despise the other. You cannot serve both God and Money."*

We have heard many people, including so-called Christians, who either don't tithe faithfully or at all, say, "I'm not giving them *my* money! I don't have enough money for me." They even say that it seems like, no matter what they do, there is always too much month left at the end of the money.

The first thing you must realize is that the tithe and offering is not about you giving to the church; it is, rather, about your faithfulness, trust and obedience to God. God said that we are to bring (not pay) all the tithe into the storehouse (the church of which you are a part) and then He will open up the windows of heaven and pour you out a blessing.

Tithing is part of being a good steward. A steward is one who manages another's property. We are merely stewards of God's property, not owners of our own. God will choose to entrust us with as much or as little as He desires. That decision will be based on how well we manage that which He has currently entrusted to us; and that begins with the tithe.

> **Luke 16:10-11** *"He that is faithful in that which is least is faithful also in much: and he that is unjust in the least is unjust also in much. If therefore ye have not been faithful in the unrighteous mammon, who will commit to your trust the true riches?"*

Quite often the demonstration of our stewardship is not in how much we give, but in how we react when we give and how we manage what is left after we give. We cannot experience peace in the area of finances until we have surrendered total control of this area to God and have accepted the role of steward.

> **1 Corinthians 4:1-2** *"Let a man regard us in this manner, as servants of Christ, and stewards of the mysteries of God....It is required of stewards that one be found trustworthy."*

Once we accept our role as stewards and manage God's resources according to His direction, He will entrust us with more and more. Often God uses money in our lives as a means of direction, because it is an area in which most of us are sensitive and vulnerable. If we are open to it, He promises to supply His wisdom and direction. But His plans for us are not always the same as our desires. Trusting God and being a good steward over that which He has entrusted to you begins with you being a joyful, faithful Tither.

> **Proverbs 3:9-10** *"[9]Honor the LORD with your wealth, with the first fruits of all your crops; [10]then your barns will be filled to overflowing, and your vats will brim over with new wine."*

Chapter 3

D. E. B. T.
(Devil's Elaborate Bondage Trap)

Debt is a serious epidemic that destroys thousands upon thousands of lives every year. Know that God does not want you to lack for anything you truly need. He wants us to have more that enough to meet our needs and the needs of others. He wants us to be lenders, not borrowers.

You no longer have to deal with the feelings that this demon called DEBT brings with it. To break this cycle from your life, begin to handle money the way the Word of God tells you to. Even if the amount of money you have never increases, if you handle it God's way, then you will have more than enough: all your needs will be met and you will have peace like never before with your finances.

Some may not admit that there's a problem, because we are ashamed to let our peers, family, or friends know that we *can't* afford the material things we have. That we *can't* afford to go shopping or out to lunch with them. That we can't even afford to put gas in the car or SUV we are driving.

Why do so many of us who are in a mess financially not look to God for help? Oh, we may pray, "God, help me out of this mess," but what we really mean is, "God, work a miracle to get me some money to fix this curse of bondage called debt that I have brought on myself."

The reason I say that that is what we are *really* saying is because we are praying for God to fix the situation – but what we should instead be praying for is the strength to fix the real problem. And that problem is us.

There are three things I want you know about debt:

1. The number one reason so many people are in such a mess financially is because they have never admitted that they are having trouble financially. Before you can solve a problem, you must first admit that you have a problem.

2. You must also understand exactly what debt is. Debt (D.E.B.T.) is the Devil's Elaborate Bondage Trap. Debt is bondage.

   Proverbs 22:7 (BBE) says, *"The man of wealth has rule over the poor, and he who gets into debt is a servant to his creditor."*

3. We get into debt because we see something that we want or think that we deserve – and borrowing is the only way we think we can get it. We sometimes try to justify it by saying that God blessed us with it.

   Proverbs 10:22 says, *"The blessing of the LORD, it maketh rich, and he addeth no sorrow with it."*

If God blesses you with something, then there will not be a struggle to keep it.

In case you are thinking or wondering whether you have a debt problem, here are just a few of many signs that might answer that question for you:

- You run out of money before you run out of month.
- You use caller ID to screen your calls for bill collectors.

- You get defensive when you and your spouse talk about money.
- You not only rob Peter to pay Paul, but you rob the rest of the disciples too.

If any of the above fits you, then you have a debt problem.

What Is Debt, Anyway?

The concept of debt is not hard to understand. Simply put, if you need money for something, you borrow that money, and you're in debt. When you give it back, you're out of debt.

> **2 Kings 6 (KJV)** 1 *And the sons of the prophets said unto Elisha, Behold now, the place where we dwell with thee is too strait for us.* 2 *Let us go, we pray thee, unto Jordan, and take thence every man a beam, and let us make us a place there, where we may dwell. And he answered, Go ye.* 3 *And one said, Be content, I pray thee, and go with thy servants. And he answered, I will go.* 4 *So he went with them. And when they came to Jordan, they cut down wood.* 5 *But as one was felling a beam, the axe head fell into the water: and he cried, and said, Alas, master! For it was borrowed.*

When we borrow something from a friend or neighbor we always try to take good care of the item. In 2 Kings 6:5, why did the son of the prophet cried out, "Alas, master! For it was borrowed!" It was because he knew that until the axe was returned, he would be in debt to its owner.

Borrowing and debt really take a turn downward when you start borrowing money and adding interest. Now when you borrow, not only do you pay back the money you borrowed, you also have to pay the lender interest on that money. If you are late with payments, then you also have to pay penalties in the form of late fees, late charges, over-the-limit charges and any other charges that the lender can come up with to increase what you owe.

What makes this type of borrowing even worse is the fact that many borrowers spend the money on things that are *wants* instead of *needs* and have only short-term benefits – things like dining out, or vacations. Then, long after that short-lived benefit is gone, you are still paying for it. Often you can't even remember what it is that you're still paying for.

History of Debt in America

The National City Bank of New York began offering loans to its working-class customers in 1928. In 1950, the original Diners Club card came about as a vision of Frank McNamara, who was part of New York's Hamilton Credit Corporation. It was a pasteboard card with the customer's name on one side and a list of the twenty-seven restaurants that accepted it on the other. In 1958, American Express began issuing credit cards, followed shortly by the Bank of America with their Bank AmeriCard, which became Visa in 1977. City Bank of New York began issuing the Everything Card in 1967, which is now known as MasterCard.

In the 1960s, with the help of the credit card, Americans began to experience what they thought was freedom to buy things with money they hadn't yet earned. Unfortunately, what seems to be freedom is actually enslavement to the lender.

"You cannot walk in Prosperity if you are in Debt"

However, it doesn't matter how convenient or how available debt is, it alone is not a problem. Debt is the *symptom* of another problem.

Philippians 4:19 (AMP) "[19]*And my God will liberally supply (fill to the full) your every need according to His riches in glory in Christ Jesus.*"

Now, if God will supply all my needs, and I am a faithful joyful Tither, why am I still struggling with paying these same bills that come at the same time every month? The simplest way I can put it is that we don't have the patience to wait for God to supply our needs ... so we finance the things we want. We have all made that mistake. It's easy to get into financial bondage.

It doesn't matter how much debt you are in, if you have faith, patience, and are willing to take the necessary steps, then you can get out of debt, no matter how much it is.

Hebrews 11:1 "*Now faith is the substance of things hoped for, the evidence of things not seen*".

Hebrews 11:6 "*But without faith it is impossible to please him: for he that cometh to God must believe that he is, and that he is a rewarder of them that diligently seek him*".

Being a Christian does not guarantee that we know how to handle money according to the word of God!

2 Kings 4:1-7 (LASB) "[1]*The wife of a man from the company of the prophets cried out to Elisha, "Your*

> *servant my husband is dead, and you know that he revered the Lord. But now his creditor is coming to take my two boys as his slaves."* [2]*Elisha replied to her, "How can I help you? Tell me, what do you have in your house?" Your servant has nothing there at all," she said, "except a little oil."* [3]*Elisha said, "Go around and ask all your neighbors for empty jars. Don't ask for just a few.* [4]*Then go inside and shut the door behind you and your sons. Pour oil into all the jars, and as each in filled, put it to one side.* [5]*She left him and afterward shut the door behind her and her sons. They brought the jars to her and she kept pouring.* [6]*When all the jars were full, she said to her son, "Bring me another one." But he replied, "There is not a jar left." Then the oil stopped flowing.* [7]*She went and told the man of God, and he said, "Go, sell the oil and pay your debts. You and your sons can live on what if left."*

In the Scripture passage above, this woman was going through a serious debt crisis; her situation was very desperate. Her husband was dead. Normally in that society, when the husband died, the sons took over the responsibility of providing for the family. But obviously, her sons were not old enough yet to take on that role. The family was in deep debt with no means to pay. The person that they owed money to was not understanding or forgiving. He had probably come to the house, banged on the door, and said something like this: "Give me my money, or tomorrow, I'm coming to get your boys and sell them as slaves!" She had lost her husband; she was getting ready to lose her children. What kept her situation from getting worse was that she sought counsel from the man of God; and when he gave her instructions about what to do she did not question them, but obeyed him instead.

We are not told in the passage exactly how this family got itself into such a mess. We do know that the father of this family had been a member of the "company of the prophets." Even though he was a godly man, that doesn't mean that he knew how to handle money well.

What is your situation? Maybe there is no one banging at your door, but are you screening your calls? Are you always paying your bills late? If so, then you are in a serious debt situation. If you're going to pay off your financial debts, you're going to have to work hard. Are you willing to be obedient to God, take the hard road, and do what He says even when it doesn't make a whole lot of sense? It doesn't make sense to go deeper in debt (borrowing jars) to pay off an existing debt. She could have said, "Wait a minute. My problem is debt, and you want me to do what?"

The issue is not whether or not it makes sense. The issue is obedience.

Chapter 4

How Too Get Out Of Debt

When we are trying to get out of a debt situation, it is necessary that we figure out how we got there to begin with. Otherwise, we will always be treating the *symptom*, rather than fixing the underlying *cause*. The problem that probably got you where you are was not a lack of funds. It was probably a failure to recognize the difference between needs and wants, and a failure to put aside resources during the good times for when the bad times would come. Until you learn to do those two things, you will always be in danger of going back into debt, regardless of how much income you have coming in.

You must learn the difference between needs and wants. And you must learn to set aside a portion of your income in preparation for the needs that you will encounter in the future. Some people are always looking for the easy way out when it comes to getting out of debt (i.e., Publishers Clearing House, tax refund, winning the lottery, bankruptcy … or God working a miracle in your creditors' computers).

If you get yourself into debt financially because of poor decisions, mismanagement of God's resources, or because you used money on selfish desires instead of meeting the needs of your family, don't expect God to work a miracle and drop money from the sky so that you can pay off your debts and never learn the lesson of responsible use of your resources!

As we said earlier, you no longer have to deal with the feelings that this demon called DEBT brings with it. To break this cycle from your life, begin to handle money the way the Word of God tells you to. Even if the amount of money you have never increases, if you handle it God's way, then you will have more that enough, all your needs will be met and you will have peace like never before with your finances.

Think about these questions:

- What brought you to the situation that you are in?
- What will you lose if your debt situation doesn't change?
- What will you gain by becoming debt-free?
- How has your debt situation affected your family?
- If you are married, how has debt affected your marriage?
- Are you willing and disciplined enough to make short-term sacrifices now for long-term rewards later?
- What resources do you have at your disposal now that might help increase your level of income?

It may seem like the only positive thing is something very insignificant, and it may take work to find it, but find it. Remember, the widow woman said, "All I've got is just this oil." However small, anything turned over to God becomes extraordinary.

To become debt-free, it will be necessary to sacrifice. It may mean repairing the washing machine instead of buying a new one. Do whatever you must to bring your debt burden under control; determine your priorities; and stick to them.

Here are 9 things you have got to do to get out of debt:

1. You have got to define the real problem.
2. You have got to make it a family effort.
3. You have got to begin with the end in mind.
4. You have got to be patient and not panic.
5. You have got to develop your own success formula.
6. You have got to be determined to make no new debt
7. You have got to look for ways to earn extra income.
8. You have got to realize that your best is good enough.
9. You have got to expect a miracle.

If you really ask God for help with your finances, He will tell you to simply apply His principles for handling money.

> **Proverbs 3:1-10, (AMP)** "[1]*MY SON, forget not my law or teaching, but let your heart keep my commandments;* [2]*For length of days and years of a life [worth living] and tranquility [inward and outward and continuing through old age till death], these shall they add to you.* [3]*Let not mercy and kindness [shutting out all hatred and selfishness] and truth [shutting out all deliberate hypocrisy or falsehood] forsake you; bind them about your neck, write them upon the tablet of your heart.* [4]*So shall you find favor, good understanding, and high esteem in the sight [or judgment] of God and man.* [5]*Lean on, trust in, and be confident in the Lord with all your heart and mind and do not rely on your own insight or understanding.* [6]*In all your ways know, recognize, and acknowledge Him, and He will direct and make straight and plain your paths.* [7]*Be not wise in your own eyes; reverently fear and worship the Lord and turn [entirely] away from evil.* [8]*It shall be health to*

your nerves and sinews, and marrow and moistening to your bones. [9]Honor the Lord with your capital and sufficiency [from righteous labors] and with the first fruits of all your income; [10]So shall your storage places be filled with plenty, and your vats shall be overflowing with new wine.

Verses 5-6 tell us that when we bring our financial needs, situations, problems, or whatever you call them to God in prayer, we must follow God's teaching. Many of us don't know how to handle money. – That is another reason you are to trust in the Lord with all your heart and lean not on your understanding; in all your ways acknowledge Him, and He will make your paths straight.

To receive God's guidance, we must acknowledge Him in all our ways. This means turning every area of our lives over to him. Look at your values and priorities. What is important to you? In what areas have you not acknowledged Him? What is His advice?

You may be acknowledging God in many areas of your life, but have you acknowledged Him in finances? By not acknowledging Him in this area, it means you are attempting to restrict or ignore His influence – and that is why you are having problems financially.

Make God a vital part of how you handle finances; then He will guide you, because you will be working to accomplish His purposes.

~~Budgeting~~

What is a budget? A budget is a plan for spending and saving your money. Making and following a budget means you can have money for the things you want. When you're not tracking your expenses, cash seems to disappear. You don't know where your money goes, and perhaps you can't afford things you'd like to have. When you know where your money goes, you feel more in control. It's easier to pay your bills on time, save money each month, and avoid money problems.

Income is the amount of money you make. Expenses are what you spend your money on. A balanced budget is when your income is at least as much as your expenses. This tool will help you balance your income.

The key to budgeting is maintaining simple but good records. Just like you did when you started your budget, you'll need to keep track of where your money comes from and where it goes. Use the system that works best for you by writing down what you spend in a notebook or keeping receipts for what you buy.

One of the easiest ways to keep track of your spending is to have a checking account. That way, when you pay for purchases with checks or your ATM or debit card, you already have a record of them. Then you only need to track a few expenses that you pay for in cash. At the end of each month, compare your actual expenses to your budget. Try to keep your spending within your plan, and look for ways to cut your expenses.

Don't give up if maintaining your budget is hard for the first few months. It may take some time to set up a plan that works for you. Be flexible. If your budget is not working for you, fix it so it will.

You may have goals and dreams, but if you don't set up guidelines for reaching them and you don't measure your progress, you will never reach them.

Before the widespread use of credit cards, you could tell if you were living within your means because you had money left over after paying all your bills. The use of credit cards has made this much less obvious. Many people don't realize they're living far beyond their means until they're knee-deep in debt.

A good budget is not just a spending plan, it's also a communication tool. Done right, a budget can bring you and your spouse closer together as you identify and work toward common goals and reduce arguments about money.

Budgeting Can Improve Your Life

1. A budget is a guide that lets you know how you're doing financially.
2. A budget lets you control your money, instead of your money controlling you.
3. A budget will help you live within your means.
4. A budget can help you meet your savings goals.
5. A budget frees up cash you didn't know you had.
6. A budget helps your family focus on common goals.
7. A budget helps you prepare for emergencies.
8. A budget reveals areas where you're spending too much money.
9. A budget can *keep* you out of debt or help you *get* out of debt.
10. A budget lets you know where your money is going.
11. A budget helps you sleep better at night.
12. A budget can improve your marriage.

~Developing A Successful Budget~

1. Teamwork: Make your budget a family project. Spouses must work together if the budget is going to be successful. Also, get your children involved and begin teaching them how to handle money properly.

2. Learn what your *true* income is. Even though you tithe on your gross income, you should set up your budget based on your net bring-home pay. This is the real money you have available to meet your monthly expenses.

3. Do your budget on a monthly basis. Prepare your budget before the month begins. List every dollar you expect to receive and then spend it all on paper. Then, when the month starts, you simply follow your plan to success.

4. Do your budget in written form! If your budget is not done in written form then you do not have a budget. You only have an idea of what to do that will never come to pass.

5. Prepare your budget in order of priority. Begin with the tithe, food, shelter, transportation and so on. Then you simply go down the list, prioritizing the next most important item as you go.

~The Checkbook~

I can tell you endless stories of Christians I know who say that they just can't use checking accounts because they don't understand how to keep them balanced. The checkbook is simply a tool that you use to transfer money from one place to another. You make a deposit into the bank and then you write a check to transfer the money to a different place. Then you just deduct that amount from your balance.

Sounds simple enough in theory, but why do so many of us have so many problems keeping the account accurate? It's because we were never taught how to properly reconcile an account, or we are just too lazy to record checks and debits at the proper time.

All checks have a set of common elements recognized around the world. Understanding how to keep a record of your checks and expenses is the fundamental concept with managing money. By being able to use and keep a checkbook balanced, you will be able to manage money, keep track of expenses, and know your spending limits.

~Elements of a Check~

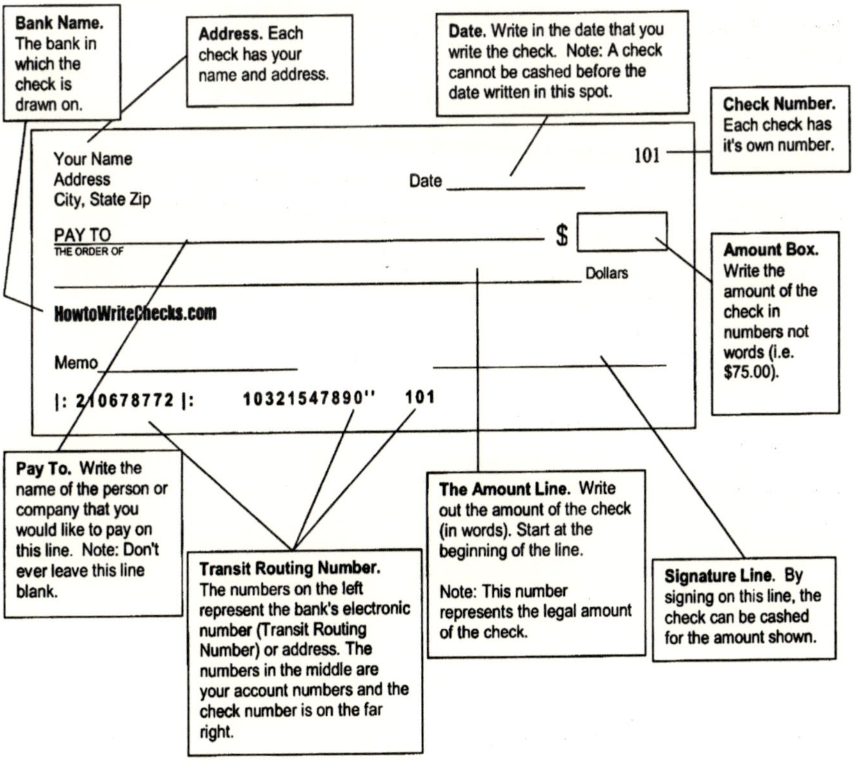

How to use the check register

The reasons for most checkbook errors include missing information, transposing of numbers, and addition and subtraction mistakes.

When using a check or your ATM card, be sure to record every transaction immediately. Use the gray shaded area in the register to record the transaction.

Even if you don't understand all the terminology associated with checking accounts, the number-one thing you must do is *record every transaction when the transaction is made*. Don't wait until later: you will forget what the transaction was for, or the transaction amount.

The second thing is to always deduct your monthly automatic payment items on time.

The third thing you must do is, every month when your bank statement comes in, is to go over it and compare it to what you have recorded in your check register.

Chapter 5

Steps to Take in Order to Repair Your Credit.

1. Make sure all current bills are paid on time every month.
2. If you see what could become a problem, you should call your creditors before they have to call you. Communication is key!
3. Know what your rights are as a borrower.
4. Learn how to read and understand a credit report.
5. Call each credit bureau to get a copy of your credit report. You can receive a free copy either by phone or on line. The relevant telephone numbers and websites are listed below.

   Equifax Information Service
   P. O. Box 740341
   Atlanta, GA 30374
   1(800) 685-1111
   equifax.com

   Experian
   P. O. Box 2002
   Allen, TX 75013
   1(888) 397-3742
   experian.com/reportaccess

   TransUnion, LLC
   P. O. Box 1000
   Chester, PA 19022
   1(866) 887-2673
   transunion.com

6. When you receive your report in the mail or receive one on line, do the following;

√Make a copy of your report; never write on the original.

√With a red pen, go through each trade line (item) for errors.

√Place an "okay" by the items that are correct.

√For the incorrect ones, write down what the error is. For example, past due amount is wrong, balance is wrong, open-since date is wrong, etc.

√Contact each credit bureau using the phone numbers provided to dispute the errors you found on the report.

√Make sure you write down the reference number they give you. You will need it when you call back to follow up.

√You should receive an updated report within three weeks; if not, contact the bureaus again.

Chapter 6

Budget Forms

Please use the following worksheets and forms as tools to help with managing your money.

Form	Use
How much money is coming in?	See at a glance all income sources and amounts you have coming into your home. It also will allow you to see what day of the month you receive it.
How much money is going out?	See at a glance how much you owe monthly to creditors. This form also shows regular living expenses. The bottom of the form is used for bad debts and collection accounts.
See how you spend your money each day?	See where you spend your money. Track for a 30 day period exactly what you spend your money on. This form will prove valuable when looking for areas to save money.
Home Budget Worksheet	Plan how you will spend your money. Without budgeting, it is impossible to keep from spending money on things that will prolong you obtaining your financial goals.
Net Income Allocation Worksheet	This form will prove to be a very useful tool. Use it to allocate money for each week so that you will see what to pay from each week's income.
Net Worth Worksheet	Use this form to see your total worth. Watch your net worth increase as you work toward your goals.

HOW MUCH MONEY IS COMING IN?

Use this form to list all income that is coming into your household, regardless of who earns it. You may be getting money from only one source or from several sources.

Where does your money come from?

Include: paycheck, commissions, child support, alimony, tax refund, insurance, social security, pension, unemployment, welfare, etc.

List what you get before any deductions (gross amount).

Source	Weekly	Bi-Monthly	Monthly	Annually

HOW MUCH MONEY IS GOING OUT?

The next part of planning, after knowing your total earnings, is to make a list of how much you have obligated on a monthly basis for debt and bills.

Let's see how much you have obligated on a monthly basis for debt. List your current debts in the top form and charged off and/or collection accounts (if any) in the bottom form.

Current Debts and Bills					
Owed To	Monthly Payment	Due Date	Interest Rate	Payments Left	Payoff Amount

Collection Accounts					
Owed To	Original Creditor	Account Number	Total Due	Settlement Amount	Date Paid Off

Let's See How You Spend

Month of ___________

Day	Ministry	Food	Bills/Debt	Housing	Health	Savings	Vehicle
1							
2							
3							
4							
5							
6							
7							
8							
9							
10							
11							
12							
13							
14							
15							
16							
17							
18							
19							
20							
21							
22							
23							
24							
25							
26							
27							
28							
29							
30							
31							

Your Money Each Day!

School	Eating Out	Entertainment	Clothing	Gifts	Other

Home Budget for the Month of ___________ : Page One				
Summary	**Budgeted**	**Actual**	**Date Due**	**Notes**
Total income				
Total expenses				
Income less expenses				

Income	**Budgeted**	**Actual**	**Date Due**	**Notes**
Salary				
Salary				
Salary				
Commission				
Tax refunds				
Social Security				
Child Support				
Pension				
Unemployment				
Welfare				
Rent				
Other				
Other				
Total income				

Ministry Expenses	**Budgeted**	**Actual**	**Date Due**	**Notes**
Tithe				
Tithe				
Offering				
Building Fund				
Church Anniversary				
Other				
Total Expenses				

Pay Yourself First	**Budgeted**	**Actual**	**Date Due**	**Notes**
Emergency Fund				
Regular Savings				
Total Savings				

Fixed Expenses	**Budgeted**	**Actual**	**Date Due**	**Notes**
Home/Renters Ins.				
Life Insurance				
Cable				
Telephone				
Cell Phone				
Other				
Other				
Other				
Total fixed expenses				

Home Budget for the Month of ______________ : Page Two				
Finance Payments	**Budgeted**	**Actual**	**Date Due**	**Notes**
Mortgage #1				
Mortgage #2				
Credit Card				
Credit Card				
Credit Card				
Car Payment				
Car Payment				
Student Loan				
Student Loan				
Other				
Other				
Other				
Other				
Total finance payments				

Variable Expenses	**Budgeted**	**Actual**	**Date Due**	**Notes**
Utilities				
Water/Sewer				
Property Taxes				
Vehicle Taxes				
Household				
Groceries				
Auto upkeep and gas				
Beauty Shop				
Clothing				
School				
Barber Shop				
School Lunches				
Memberships				
Dining out				
Allowance				
Allowance				
Other				
Other				
Total variable expenses				

Debt Snowball	**Budgeted**	**Actual**	**Date Due**	**Notes**
Total Debt Snowball				

Net Income Allocation Worksheet

		INCOME SOURCE/PAY PERIOD				
Budget Item	**Monthly Allocation**	**1st Week**	**2nd Week**	**3rd Week**	**4th Week**	**5th Week**
1.						
2.						
3.						
4.						
5.						
6.						
7.						
8.						
9.						
10.						
11.						
12.						
13.						
14.						
15.						
16.						
17.						
18.						
19.						
20.						
21.						
22.						
23.						
24.						
25.						
26.						
27.						
28.						

Net Worth Worksheet

Column A		Column B	
Assets		**Liabilities**	
Personal Items	**Est. Value**	**Loan Balances**	**Est. Value**
Home		Mortgage loan	
Vehicles		Home equity	
Jewelry		Car loans	
Artwork		Real estate	
Furniture		Student loans	
Electronics		Other loans	
Antiques			
Other			
Cash or Cash Equivalent		**Other Outstanding Debt**	
Checking account		Credit card debt	
Savings account		Other debt	
Certificates of deposit			
Money market account			
Life insurance (cash value)			
Other			
Investments			
Retirement account			
Bonds			
Mutual funds			
Individual stock shares			
Rental Property			
Other-			
Other-			
Assets Total	$	**Liabilities Total**	$

Column B	
Assets Total	$
- Liabilities Total	$
= Net Worth	$

Matthew 16:26 (NLT) *"And how do you benefit if you gain the whole world but lose your own soul in the process? Is anything worth more than your soul?"*

We truly believe and stand by that Scripture. God has blessed us abundantly and we owe it all to Him, because He tore down and reshaped our entire lives over six years ago. Because of what we went through and came out of with joy, God has entrusted His finances and financial wisdom with us. He has also given us the ability to teach others how to manage their personal finances, live on a budget, get out – and stay out – of debt.

We reside in Wilson, North Carolina and attend New Fellowship Center of Refuge, under the leadership of Cathy Farmer, Pastor and Overseer.

Laura wholes a B.A. Degree from Jackson State University in Jackson, MS and works for a large national bank. Kevin graduated from the Electronic Computer Programming Institute in Virginia Beach, VA and is a Sales Account Executive for an office equipment dealership. We are also the owners of a promotional advertising agency, Spirit-Filled Creative Designs. For more information you can reach us @ www.spiritfilledcreativedesigns.com

Family is very important to us. That's one of the reasons why we are so thankful for our parents: Ivory and Janice Hinnant *(Kevin)* of Wilson, NC; Verna Mae Jimmerson *(Laura)* of Belzoni, MS; and our spiritual mother, Sarah Cathy Farmer of Wilson, NC. We have also been blessed with four children: Lakisha, Cory, Kevin Jr., and Pashion; a very special niece, Veronica; and many special family members and friends.

Kevin and Laura Hinnant

More From Dream Books

From Crack Addict To Pastor a true story by Karen Sills ISBN 0-9770936-3-8

Pastor Karen Sills describes her years of substance abuse in this dramatized rendition of her life. She gives detailed accounts of how drug addiction impacted her and the lives of the people she loves dearly. Through this book she shows just how merciful God is. And because of His mercy and grace, she is delivered from prostitution, lesbianism, imprisonment and drug addiction.

Perfect Love
a novel by Arsoleen Woolcock
ISBN 0-9770936-4-6

Breanna's one dream is to find that special love by a man who's as wonderful as her father. But the secret that has been hidden for years surfaces likely to destroy her dreams of forever after in a Perfect Love.

The Homecoming (Mt. Hope Series Book #1)
a novel by Angela Santana ISBN 0-9770936-7-0

Tragedy turns to blessing when a despondent, desperate young pioneer woman finds herself alone and in crisis in an unfamiliar place. Faced with a decision she never thought she'd have to make, she learns that God's grace is not just sufficient but abounding, and that all things work together for good if only she can learn to trust…

Victory Day By Day by Dr. Arlene H. Churn ISBN 0-9770936-8-9

Victory Day By Day is a personal collection of affirmations for achieving and living a victorious life through the spoken word. It is meant to increase the faith of the reader and to fortify them with vocal power over life's daily adversities and challenges. Victory is achieved gradually, day by day, and each victory will lead to spiritual growth with unlimited possibilities. Keep VICTORY IN YOUR VIEW

Name____

Address____

City___________________________State_______Zip____________

Please send me the books I have checked below.

___**Perfect Love**
a novel by Arsoleen Woolcock
ISBN 0-9770936-4-6
$13.99 USA $21.99 CAN

___**From Crack Addict To Pastor**
a true story by Karen Sills
ISBN 0-9770936-3-8
$12.00 USA $19.00 CAN

___**The Homecoming**
Angela Santana
ISBN 0-9770936-7-0
$13.99 USA $21.99 CAN

___**Victory Day By Day**
by Rev. Dr. Arlene H. Churn
ISBN 0-9770936-8-9
$6.99 USA $10.99 CAN
I am enclosing $________________

Plus postage & handling $________________

Total amount enclosed $________________

*Add $2.65 for the first book and $.60 for each additional book. Send Money Order. (No Cash, C.O.D. or Personal Checks) to Dreams Publishing Co. P.O. Box 4731, Rocky Mount, NC 27801.

Price and Numbers subject to change without notice. All orders subject to availability.

Check out: www.DreamsPublishing.com

The Dilemma's Series by Reign

Book #1

Book #2

The Dilemma's Series are stories base around Ivy Jones-Miller, Sheena Daniels, Miranda Jones and Jade Sanders. Each woman tackle trials and tribulations and winning against all odds though their faith in God and love and devotion of friendship. Books In The Dilemma Series: "Ivy's Dilemma (Thy Will Be Done)" published 2005 "Jade's Dilemma (Lead Us Not Into Temptation)" published 2006 and "Sheena's Dilemma (It's Better To Marry Than to Burn) not yet published.

Call toll free: 1-877-209-5200 to order by phone or use this coupon to order by mail.

Name____
Address____
City______________________State________Zip____________
Please send me the books I have checked below.

___Ivy's Dilemma – Thy Will Be Done
ISBN 0-9770936-0-3
$12.00 USA $19.00 CAN

___Jade's Dilemma – Lead Us Not Into Temptation
ISBN 0-9770936-5-4
$12.00 USA $19.00 CAN

I am enclosing $_______________ Plus postage & handling
$_______________ Total amount enclosed $_______________

*Add $2.65 for the first book and $.60 for each additional book. Send Money Order. (No Cash, C.O.D. or Personal Checks) to Dreams Publishing Co. P.O. Box 4731, Rocky Mount, NC 27801.
Price and Numbers subject to change without notice. All orders subject to availability.

Printed in the United States
76061LV00006B/277-351

9 780977 093694